Classic Recipes of the
PHILIPPINES

Classic Recipes of the
PHILIPPINES

TRADITIONAL FOOD AND COOKING
IN 25 AUTHENTIC DISHES

GHILLIE BAŞAN AND VILMA LAUS
PHOTOGRAPHY BY MARTIN BRIGDALE

LORENZ BOOKS

This edition is published by
Lorenz Books,
an imprint of Anness Publishing Ltd,
108 Great Russell Street,
London WC1B 3NA

www.lorenzbooks.com;
www.annesspublishing.com

If you like the images in this book and
would like to investigate using them for
publishing, promotions or advertising,
please visit our website
www.practicalpictures.com for more
information.

Publisher: Joanna Lorenz
Editors: Lucy Doncaster & Helen Sudell
Designer: Nigel Partridge
Recipe Photography: Martin Brigdale
Home Economist: Lucy McKelvie
Stylist: Helen Trent
Production Controller: Rosanna Anness

PUBLISHER'S NOTE
Although the advice and information in this
book are believed to be accurate and true
at the time of going to press, neither the
authors nor the publisher can accept any
legal responsibility or liability for any errors
or omissions that may have been made nor
for any inaccuracies nor for any loss, harm
or injury that comes about from following
instructions or advice in this book.

These recipes were originally published as
part of a larger volume, *The Food and
Cooking of Indonesia and the Philippines*.

PUBLISHER'S ACKNOWLEDGEMENTS
The Publisher would like to thank the
following agencies for the use of their
images. Alamy: p6, p11 (both), p13.
Fotalia p6. Istock: p8, p10.

COOK'S NOTES
Bracketed terms are intended for American
readers. For all recipes, quantities are given
in both metric and imperial measures and,
where appropriate, in standard cups and
spoons. Follow one set of measures, but
not a mixture, because they are not
interchangeable.

Standard spoon and cup measures are
level. 1 tsp = 5ml, 1 tbsp = 15ml, 1 cup =
250ml/8fl oz. Australian standard
tablespoons are 20ml. Australian readers
should use 3 tsp in place of 1 tbsp for
measuring small quantities.

American pints are 16fl oz/2 cups.
American readers should use 20fl oz/2.5
cups in place of 1 pint when measuring
liquids.

Electric oven temperatures in this book are
for conventional ovens. When using a fan
oven, the temperature will probably need to
be reduced by about 10–20°C/20–40°F.
Since ovens vary, you should check with
your manufacturer's instruction book for
guidance.

The nutritional analysis given for each
recipe is calculated per portion (i.e. serving
or item), unless otherwise stated. If the
recipe gives a range, such as Serves 4–6,
then the nutritional analysis will be for the
smaller portion size, i.e. 6 servings. The
analysis does not include optional
ingredients, such as salt added to taste.

Medium (US large) eggs are used unless
otherwise stated.

Contents

Introduction

The islands of the Philippines lie around 800km/500 miles south-east of the Asian continent and are renowned for their beauty, with palm-fringed beaches and stunning reefs. Surrounded by oceans and criss-crossed by rivers and streams, it is inevitable that the cuisine draws heavily from the ocean. The tropical climate means a harvest rich in fruits and herbs. In addition to an abundance of fresh food, the Philippines is also a melting pot of cultural and geographical influences, from as far afield as China and Spain, making the food and cooking of the Philippines a unique experience. Popular ingredients include chilli, galangal, garlic and shrimp paste, which are balanced by the use of peanuts and coconut milk to create a perfect harmony of taste and texture.

Left: Rice paddie fields in the northern Philippines. Rice is a staple food for Filipinos.

Filipino Cuisine

As in the rest of South-east Asia, rice is the staple food of the Philippines and is served with almost every dish. Fried rice is served for breakfast, along with dried fish or longaniza, the local spicy pork sausages. Fried eggs are popular for breakfast too.

Although the morning *merienda* is referred to as a snack, it can range from something as simple as a few slices of watermelon to a filling bowl of stir-fried noodles,

Below: Fresh vegetables at a street market stall.

spring rolls or even an array of savoury sandwiches and sweet, sticky rice cakes.

Lunch and supper tend to be big meals in the Philippines. Between lunch and supper there is yet another merienda, which consists of sandwiches, cakes and tea, but also spring rolls (*lumpia*), noodles (*pancit*) and a few local sweet dishes made from coconut milk, glutinous rice, pineapple or other tropical fruits.

Foods and techniques
Traditionally, roasting, steaming and sautéing are the main methods used for cooking fish and meat. Fish is also marinated in sour flavours which are sourced naturally from fruits such as tamarind, guava and kalamansi limes.

Salty flavours are derived from the national fermented fish sauces, patis and bagoong, and from Chinese soy sauce, whereas the sweet notes come from blocks of natural palm sugar. Meat, though much sought after, is

eaten less frequently because of the cost. However, when it comes to fiestas and family celebrations, no expense is spared with every imaginable meat dish being on offer.

At a meal, food is often laid out buffet-style in a colourful display. The rich Spanish-influenced dishes are often quite filling, but interspersed among them are lighter dishes, such as fried prawns (shrimp) and vegetables in a tamarind-flavoured broth, and tangy seaweed and freshly prepared papaya salads.

Thanks to the Spanish, bread plays an important role in Filipino meals, where it is called *pain de sal* and is made with salt, sugar and wheat flour to produce a spongy baked bun that is dipped in hot coffee or tea. As well as rice, the daily appearance of bread in the Philippines is quite unusual in South-east Asia.

Right: Spring rolls and noodles are foods often enjoyed at the afternoon merienda.

Feasts and Festivals

The 400-year occupation of the Philippines by the Spanish had a lasting impact on cultural life with Filipinos embracing the Catholic faith. Today, the Philippines is the only Christian country in Asia. With the faith came religious festivals and festive dishes, which are mainly of Spanish origin but with a native twist.

Filipino fiestas

There are plenty of occasions to celebrate in the Philippines, as the festivals range from religious and communal get-togethers to the full-blown,

Below: Festival masks on a street stall in Manila.

week-long Mardi Gras, *Ati-Atihan*, which rivals the carnival in Rio de Janeiro for vibrancy and takes place in towns such as Kalibo and Makato, starting on the third Sunday of January.

Another Mardi Gras-style festival takes place in Iloilo City and celebrates the patron saint, Santo Nino, with a procession of outrageous costumes, dancing and plenty of food. In October, there is a wonderful food festival in Zamboanga city. With street parties, food fairs, open markets, dancing and a regatta with traditional sailboats, this is a colourful extravaganza.

Feast days

Every town in the Philippines has a patron saint, and each town has a feast day to celebrate its founding anniversary. This means that there is always a fiesta somewhere in the Philippines. Floats are decorated with flowers and images of the village royalty, and people dress in historical costume and

Above: Flan is a popular festival dessert in the Philippines.

hold dancing competitions. Special dishes, such as adobo, are prepared and shared among neighbours.

Many of the festive foods on these occasions are Spanish in origin, and include savoury favourites, such as *pochero* (beef and chorizo stew with plantain and chickpeas), and sweet dishes, such as *leche flan* (Filipino crème caramel). Chinese-inspired noodle dishes, such as *pancit guisado* (stir-fried noodles), *pancit luglog* (noodle soup) and *pancit molo* (a Filipino version of wonton soup), are also popular festive dishes.

All Saints Day

For All Saints Day on 1 November families gather at the local cemetery to feast on the favourite dishes of the deceased, snacking and celebrating long into the night by the gravesides, to the sound of guitars.

Christmas and New Year

The advent of Christmas and New Year are great occasions for celebrating with food. Generally, if a Filipino lives near a beach, the fiesta will take place there. Lots of pork and chicken dishes, such as *aroz*

Below: A suckling pig is the highlight of many Filipino feasts.

Above: Young girls enjoy the Mardi Gras festivities.

valenciana (Filipino risotto with stir-fried liver), paella and adobo are prepared, as well as a spit-roast suckling pig and vast quantities of rice cakes.

New Year welcomes the abundance of produce in the coming year. To mark the occasion, Filipinos prepare satay and fruit salads, which include more expensive fruits, such as grapes and apples, and there are lantern processions in every village.

Easter

Filipinos look forward to the Easter festival most since everyone goes to the beach with lots of food to share. During the Holy Week, when the Filipinos fast for five days, they are only allowed to eat fish and vegetables in the morning and evening. Between 12 noon and 5pm, they must fast. The feasting on the Sunday, the Day of the Resurrection, is inevitably spectacular. There is always a suckling pig roasting on a spit, plus many other pork dishes.

Classic Ingredients

The food of the Philippines differs from that of the rest of South-east Asia primarily in that it does not rely heavily on herbs and spices. It is founded instead on ginger, onion, and garlic, combining the cooking methods of the colonial Spaniards with the traditional dishes of the indigenous island people. The result is a hearty and simple cuisine that makes good use of innards and oxtail, as well as insects and crickets from the rice paddies.

Below: Finger chillies are often served for guests to chew on.

The Spanish style of *la cocina Filipina* makes the most of an interesting mix of local ingredients, which are often sautéed and casseroled. A rounded pan, the carajay, which is shaped like a wok, is used for stir-frying ingredients, such as vegetables and noodles, but the majority of the cooking is done in frying pans and casseroles.

The Filipinos also enjoy a fiery burst of chillies but they are not always included in the dish. Instead hot Thai chillies, or finger chillies as they are known in the Philippines, are offered to chew on, or they are chopped finely and used to spike the beloved coconut vinegar that is splashed on to dishes and offered as a dip.

Sauces and marinades

The Filipinos have their own version of shrimp paste, which is called bagoong. More of a sauce than a paste, the fermented *bagoong* is sold in bottles in which you can actually see the tiny shrimp or anchovies floating. The sauce is a greyish, opaque colour with a very strong smell and is an acquired taste.

Dearly treasured by Filipinos, bagoong is more often reserved for particular dishes, such as *pinakbet* (aubergine, bitter melon and okra stew), whereas the pungent, national fish sauce, *patis*, is used in almost everything. Both are available in South-east Asian and Chinese markets but, as an alternative, you can substitute bagoong with Chinese anchovy sauce.

Filipinos frequently draw on the Spanish love of marinades. Ingredients are often marinated in coconut vinegar, ginger and garlic before cooking, and raw ingredients such as oily fish and shrimp are cured in lime juice and coconut vinegar, as exemplified in the national favourite kinilaw (Filipino cured herring).

Right: Local fishermen near the coastal town of Puerto Galera, Mindoro Island.

Above: Kalamansi limes are native to the Philippines.

Sweet and sour

Herbs and strong spices are used sparingly in Filipino cooking, which relies mainly on garlic, ginger and bay leaves for flavouring. The Filipino penchant for sweet and sour notes is achieved by combining coconut vinegar or kalamansi lime juice with palm or cane sugar, as in adobo (chicken and pork cooked with vinegar and ginger), the national dish, which originally hailed from Mexico.

When Filipinos talk about their beloved vinegar they mean coconut vinegar, which is cloudy white and made from coconut palm sap. Generally, they prefer to cook with coconut oil, or with groundnut or corn oils for frying.

Garnishes

The Filipino culture strives for balance in its meals and regards the finishing touches as extremely important. Garnishes, such as fried shallots, spring onions (scallions) and sprigs of coriander (cilantro) are not just for decorative purposes, they are very much part of the dish as a whole and should not be omitted.

Below: Fresh coriander leaves add colour and taste to a dish.

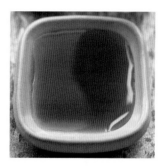

Above: Salty, tangy patis is used often in Filipino cooking.

Dips, sauces and sambals are equally important to Filipino cuisine, and are considered crucial to the whole enjoyment of a particular dish. For example, most fried fish in the Philippines would be regarded as naked and dull without a liberal sprinkling of the fish sauce *patis*.

When it comes to street food, however, traditions can go haywire in some areas, as tomato ketchup appears with increasing frequency in the more Americanized bars and stalls in the cities of Manila and Cebu.

Kalamansi sauce
Sawsawan kalamansi

This popular Filipino dipping sauce can be served with anything, but is particularly good with fish and rice dishes.

Serves 4
2 kalamansi limes
60ml/4 tbsp patis (fish sauce)

1 Squeeze the juice from the limes and put in a small bowl. Add the patis and beat together until thoroughly blended.

2 Spoon the sauce into a jar, cover and store in the refrigerator for up to 1–2 days.

Tamarind and lime sauce
Sampaloc at kalamansi

This hot and sour dipping sauce is usually prepared for freshly grilled fish or steamed shellfish.

Serves 4
2 kalamansi limes
30ml/2 tbsp tamarind paste
2 spring onions (scallions), white
   parts only, finely chopped
2 red chillies, seeded and finely
   chopped

1 Squeeze the juice from the limes and put in a small bowl. Add the tamarind paste and mix together. Add a little water to thin the mixture until it is of dipping consistency. Stir in the spring onions and chillies.

2 Spoon the sauce into a jar, cover and store in the refrigerator for up to 1 week.

COOK'S TIP
If you cannot obtain tamarind sauce, replace it with lime juice, mixed with an equal quantity of light brown sugar for that sweet and sour effect.

Coconut vinegar sauce
Sukat bawang sawsawan

This spicy dipping sauce is perfect with steamed shellfish, spring rolls and fried chicken.

Serves 4
60–75ml/4–5 tbsp coconut vinegar
3 red chillies, seeded and finely
   chopped
4 spring onions (scallions), white
   parts only, finely chopped
4 garlic cloves, finely chopped

1 Spoon the vinegar into a small bowl. Add the chillies, spring onions and garlic and mix well.

2 Spoon the sauce into a jar, cover and store in the refrigerator for up to 1 week.

Filipino Flavours

The food culture of the Philippines is generally a healthy one based on plenty of rice, fresh fish and a wide range of seasonal vegetables, which includes both indigenous ingredients and those that were brought over by settlers. This eclectic mix of culinary traditions is celebrated here with warming soups, hot street snacks and nourishing rice and noodle dishes. Other recipes celebrate the Filipino love of spicy fish, roast meats, and fragrant salads. A delicious selection of sweet snacks and drinks complete this collection of recipes from across the islands.

Left: Fresh fruit and vegetables feature prominently in the Filipino diet.

Chicken and Ginger Broth with Papaya Tinolang manok

1 Heat the oil in a wok or a large pan that has a lid. Stir in the garlic, onion and ginger and fry until they begin to colour. Stir in the chillies, add the chicken and fry until the skin is lightly browned all over.

2 Pour in the *patis*, stock and water, adding more water if necessary so that the chicken is completely covered. Bring to the boil, reduce the heat, cover and simmer gently for about 1½ hours, until the chicken is very tender.

3 Season the stock with salt and pepper and add the papaya. Continue to simmer for a further 10–15 minutes, then stir in the chilli or basil leaves. Serve the chicken and broth in warmed bowls, with bowls of steamed rice to ladle the broth over the top.

VARIATION
Young chilli leaves, plucked off the chilli plant, are added at the end to spike the soup with their unique flavour. There is no similar substitute for these leaves, but if you don't have any, you can use fresh Thai basil instead.

Serves 4–6
15–30ml/1–2 tbsp palm or
  groundnut (peanut) oil
2 garlic cloves, finely chopped
1 large onion, sliced
40g/1½oz fresh root ginger,
  finely grated
2 whole dried chillies
1 chicken, left whole or jointed,
  trimmed of fat
30ml/2 tbsp *patis* (fish sauce)
600ml/1 pint/2½ cups chicken stock
1.2 litres/2 pints/5 cups water
1 small green papaya, cut into fine
  slices or strips
1 bunch fresh young chilli or basil
  leaves
salt and ground black pepper
cooked rice, to serve

In the Philippines, this is a traditional peasant dish that is still cooked every day in rural areas. In the province of Iloilo, located in the Western Visayas, green papaya is added to the broth, which could be regarded as a Filipino version of coq au vin. Generally, the chicken and broth are served with steamed rice, but the broth is also sipped during the meal to cleanse and stimulate the palate.

Rice Soup with Pork and Roasted Garlic
Arroz caldo at baboy

Serves 4–6

15–30ml/1–2 tbsp palm or
    groundnut (peanut) oil
1 large onion, finely chopped
2 garlic cloves, finely chopped
25g/1oz fresh root ginger, finely
    chopped
350g/12oz pork rump or tenderloin,
    cut widthways into bitesize slices
5–6 black peppercorns
115g/4oz/1 cup plus 15ml/1 tbsp
    short grain rice
2 litres/3½ pints/8 cups pork or
    chicken stock
30ml/2 tbsp *patis* (fish sauce)
salt

To serve

2 garlic cloves, finely chopped
2 spring onions (scallions), white
    parts only, finely sliced
2–3 green or red chillies, seeded
    and quartered lengthways

1 Heat the oil in a wok or deep, heavy pan that has a lid. Stir in the onion, garlic and ginger and fry until fragrant and beginning to colour. Add the pork and fry, stirring frequently, for 5–6 minutes, until lightly browned. Stir in the peppercorns.

2 Meanwhile, put the rice in a sieve or strainer, rinse under cold running water until the water runs clear, then drain. Toss the rice into the pan, making sure that it is coated in the mixture. Pour in the stock, add the *patis* and bring to the boil. Reduce the heat and partially cover with a lid. Simmer for about 40 minutes, stirring ocasionally to make sure that the rice doesn't stick to the bottom of the pan. Season with salt to taste.

3 Just before serving, dry-fry the garlic in a small, heavy pan, until golden brown, then stir it into the soup. Ladle the soup into individual warmed bowls and sprinkle the spring onions over the top. Serve the chillies separately, to chew on.

Made with pork or chicken, this warming and sustaining rice soup combines the ancient traditions of the Filipino rice culture with the Spanish colonial culinary techniques of browning and sautéing.

Pork Satay Baboy satay

Serves 4

30ml/2 tbsp groundnut (peanut)
    or palm oil
60–75ml/4–5 tbsp soy sauce
15ml/1 tbsp *patis* (fish sauce)
juice of 2–3 kalamansi or
    ordinary limes
2 garlic cloves, crushed
15ml/1 tbsp palm, granulated
    or muscovado sugar
500g/1¼lb pork loin, cut into thin
    bitesize squares
175g/6oz slim chorizo sausage,
    sliced diagonally
12 baby onions, peeled and
    left whole
ground black pepper
wooden or metal skewers

To serve

cooked rice
salad or pickled vegetables
coconut vinegar sauce

*This is the most popular of
all the satay dishes in the
Philippines. Pork is the
favoured meat and satay is
a beautifully simple way of
cooking it.*

1 In a large bowl, mix the oil, soy sauce, *patis*, lime juice, garlic and sugar together to form a marinade. Stir well to ensure the sugar dissolves and season with black pepper.

2 Toss the meat in the marinade, making sure that it is well coated. Cover the bowl with clear film (plastic wrap) and put in the refrigerator for at least 2 hours or overnight. (The longer the pork is marinated the better the flavour.)

3 Prepare the barbecue, or, if you are using a grill (broiler), preheat 5 minutes before you start cooking. If using wooden skewers, soak them in water for about 30 minutes. Thread the meat, chorizo and onions on to the skewers and place them on the barbecue or under the hot grill.

4 Cook the satay for 4–5 minutes each side, basting the meat with the marinade occasionally. Serve immediately with rice and a salad or pickled vegetables, and a bowl of coconut vinegar dipping sauce.

Crispy Fried Pork Belly Bagnet

Serves 4

3 garlic cloves, chopped
40g/1½oz fresh root ginger, chopped
500g/1¼lb pork belly with the rind,
   cut into thick slabs
3–4 bay leaves
corn, groundnut (peanut) or
   vegetable oil, for deep-frying
salt and ground black pepper

This is a great Filipino treat. Delicious and moreish, the crispy pork can be sliced and eaten as a snack with pickles, or it can be added to salads, soups and vegetable dishes.

1 Using a mortar and pestle, grind the garlic and ginger with a little salt and pepper, until the mixture forms a fairly smooth paste. Rub the paste all over the pork slabs and put them on a plate. Cover with clear film (plastic wrap) and put in the refrigerator to marinate for at least 1 hour or overnight.

2 Fill a pan with water and bring to the boil. Add the bay leaves, reduce the heat and slip in the marinated pork slabs. Cook gently for about 1 hour, until the meat is tender but still firm. Using a colander, drain the slabs and leave them in the colander for 30–40 minutes to dry out.

3 Heat enough oil in a wok or pan for deep-frying. Fry the pork for 5 minutes, until they are golden brown. Using a slotted spoon, lift them out and drain on kitchen paper. If eating immediately, slice thinly and serve with rice and pickled vegetables. Alternatively, store in the refrigerator for up to 5 days to use in soups and stews.

Spanish-style Omelette with Bitter Melon
Guisadong ampalya at itlog

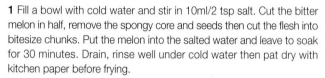

Serves 3–4

450g/1lb bitter melon
30–45ml/2–3 tbsp palm or
   groundnut (peanut) oil
1 onion, sliced
2–3 garlic cloves, chopped
25g/1oz fresh root ginger, chopped
115g/4oz pork loin, cut into thin
   bitesize strips
225g/8oz fresh shrimp or small
   prawns (shrimp), shelled
2–3 tomatoes, skinned, seeded
   and chopped
1 small bunch chilli leaves or flat leaf
   parsley, roughly chopped
3–4 eggs, beaten
salt and ground black pepper

1 Fill a bowl with cold water and stir in 10ml/2 tsp salt. Cut the bitter melon in half, remove the spongy core and seeds then cut the flesh into bitesize chunks. Put the melon into the salted water and leave to soak for 30 minutes. Drain, rinse well under cold water then pat dry with kitchen paper before frying.

2 Heat the oil in a large frying pan, stir in the onion, garlic and ginger and fry until fragrant and beginning to colour. Add the pork and fry for 2 minutes.

3 Add the shrimp and fry until they turn opaque, then add the tomatoes and chilli leaves or parsley. Toss in the bitter melon and fry for 3–4 minutes, until tender. Season the mixture with salt and pepper.

4 Pour the eggs over the mixture in the pan, drawing in the sides to let the egg spread evenly. Cover the pan and leave to cook gently until the eggs have set.

5 Serve the omelette hot, straight from the pan, or leave it to cool and serve it at room temperature.

VARIATION
Bitter melon is available in Chinese and South-east Asian markets but if you have any trouble finding one, you could use courgette (zucchini) as a substitute.

*Bitter melon, which is also known as bitter gourd
or bitter cucumber, is best eaten when it is young.
Made in the style of a Spanish omelette, this
Filipino dish is often enjoyed as a snack, served
on a banana leaf with rice or bread.*

Fried Rice with Chorizo and Fried Eggs Sinangag

1 Heat 15–30ml/1–2 tbsp of the oil in a wok or heavy pan, stir in the garlic and fry until fragrant and golden brown. Toss in the rice, breaking up any lumps, and add the *patis*. Season the rice with salt to taste, if needed, and black pepper. Turn off the heat and cover the wok or pan to keep the rice warm.

2 In a heavy frying pan, heat 15ml/1 tbsp of the oil, add the sliced chorizo and fry until crispy on both sides. Drain the chorizo on kitchen paper.

3 Heat the remaining 15–30ml/1–2 tbsp oil in a separate frying pan and fry the eggs, sunny-side up for 1–2 minutes. Alternatively, fry the eggs over-easy, cooking them in the same way as sunny-side up then carefully turning the eggs over and frying for no more than 30 seconds until a film is set over the yolk without browning.

4 Spoon the rice on to individual serving plates. Alternatively, pack the rice into a cup or bowl and invert each portion of rice on to plates. Place the fried eggs on top of the rice and arrange the chorizo around the edge. Serve warm with the coconut vinegar.

COOK'S TIP
If you don't have any cooked, leftover rice, cook 225g/8oz/1 cup rice, allow to cool and use in the same way as leftover rice.

This rice dish is often eaten at breakfast. To make a substantial meal to start the day, it is served at street stalls and cafés with fried dried fish, such as the crispy danggit from Cebu, fried eggs, pork jerky or the spicy sausage, longaniza, which can be substituted with the similar-tasting Spanish chorizo. This delicious recipe is a great way of using up leftover rice.

Serves 4

45–75ml/3–5 tbsp palm, groundnut (peanut) or vegetable oil
2–3 garlic cloves, crushed
450g/1lb cooked long grain rice
15–30ml/1–2 tbsp *patis* (fish sauce)
2 small, thin chorizo sausages, about 175g/6oz each, sliced diagonally
4 eggs
salt and ground black pepper
coconut vinegar, to serve

Paella Paella

1 Put the rice in a sieve or strainer, rinse under cold running water until the water runs clear then drain. Heat the oil in a wok or wide, shallow heavy pan with a lid. Add the chicken drumsticks and wings and fry for about 5 minutes, until browned on both sides. Remove the chicken from the pan and put aside.

2 Add the onion, garlic and ginger to the pan and fry until fragrant and beginning to colour. Add the paprika, tomato purée, bay leaves and drained rice and toss in the chicken. Pour in the stock and bring to the boil. Add the *patis* and season with salt and lots of black pepper. Cover the pan and simmer gently for 15–20 minutes, until the rice and chicken are almost cooked.

3 Toss in the peas and add the prawns and clams, sitting them on top of the rice. Cover the pan again and cook for a further 10 minutes or until all the liquid has evaporated. Serve warm with kalamansi sauce and a bowl of sliced chillies.

COOK'S TIPS
To make a perfect paella, it is essential to have a very wide, shallow, heavy pan with a lid.
Take care to discard any clams that are open before cooking or remain closed after cooking.

Serves 6
500g/1¼lb/2½ cups long grain rice
45–60ml/3–4 tbsp palm or
    groundnut (peanut) oil
12 chicken drumsticks and wings
2 onions, finely chopped
4 garlic cloves, finely chopped
40g/1½oz fresh root ginger, chopped
5ml/1 tsp paprika
30–45ml/2–3 tbsp tomato purée
    (paste)
2–3 bay leaves
1.2 litres/2 pints/5 cups chicken
    stock
15–30ml/1–2 tbsp *patis* (fish sauce)
400g/14oz can petit pois
    (baby peas), drained
12 prawns (shrimp) in their shells,
    cleaned and rinsed
12 medium clams, cleaned and
    rinsed
salt and ground black pepper

To serve
4 red chillies, seeded and quartered
kalamansi sauce

Strikingly similar to Spanish paella and called by the same name, the Filipino version is packed with crabs, clams and prawns, although any shellfish can be used, and flavoured with ginger and bay leaves.

Risotto with Stir-fried Liver Aroz valenciana

Serves 3–4

225g/8oz/generous 1 cup sticky or glutinous rice
900ml/1½ pints pork or chicken stock
45–60ml/3–4 tbsp groundnut (peanut) or vegetable oil
3–4 shallots, finely chopped
3 garlic cloves, finely chopped
25g/1oz fresh root ginger, finely chopped
25g/1oz fresh turmeric, finely chopped
175g/6oz/¾ cup small raisins or currants
225g/8oz pork fillet, cut into thin bitesize strips
450g/1lb pig's liver, cut into bitesize strips
30–45ml/2–3 tbsp rice flour or plain (all-purpose) white flour
salt and ground black pepper

To serve

45–60ml/3–4 tbsp roasted, unsalted peanuts, crushed
2 hard-boiled eggs, quartered
2–3 spring onions (scallions), white parts only, sliced
2 red or green chillies, seeded and quartered lengthways
coconut vinegar

1 Put the rice in a sieve or strainer, rinse under cold running water until the water runs clear, then drain. Pour the stock into a pan and bring it to the boil. Make sure it is well seasoned, and then reduce the heat and leave to simmer.

2 Meanwhile, heat 30ml/2 tbsp of the oil in a wok or heavy pan, stir in the shallots, garlic, ginger and turmeric and fry until fragrant and beginning to colour. Add the raisins or currants and toss in the pork. Stir-fry for 2–3 minutes, until the pork is well browned. Toss in the rice, making sure that it is thoroughly mixed.

3 Gradually add ladlefuls of the hot stock to the rice and, stirring from time to time, cook over a medium heat until the liquid has been absorbed before adding another ladleful. When all the stock has been added, cover the pan and leave to cook gently, until almost all the liquid has been absorbed.

4 Meanwhile, toss the liver in the flour. Just before the rice is cooked, heat the remaining oil in a frying pan. Add the liver and stir-fry for 2–3 minutes. Season the liver with salt and pepper.

5 Tip the risotto into a warmed serving dish. Spoon the liver on top and scatter over the ground peanuts. Arrange the chopped eggs, spring onions and chillies around the dish and serve immediately with the coconut vinegar.

It's not hard to guess the origins of this recipe! Made in a similar way to Italian risotto, the rice and pork are cooked in stock that is added gradually. This type of rice dish is usually served as a snack and much enjoyed at Christmas and Easter, when a vast number of pork-based dishes are cooked and shared with neighbours.

Celebration Noodles Pancit palabok

Serves 4

30ml/2 tbsp palm or coconut oil
1 large onion, finely chopped
2–3 garlic cloves, finely chopped
250g/9oz pork loin, cut into thin
 strips
250g/9oz fresh shelled shrimp
2 carrots, cut into matchsticks
½ small green cabbage, finely
 shredded
about 250ml/8fl oz/1 cup pork or
 chicken stock
50ml/2fl oz/¼ cup soy sauce
15ml/1 tbsp palm sugar
450g/1lb fresh egg noodles
2 hard-boiled eggs, finely chopped
1 lime, quartered

1 Heat 15ml/1 tbsp oil in a wok or a large, heavy frying pan, stir in the onion and garlic and fry until fragrant and beginning to colour. Toss in the pork and shrimp and stir-fry for 2 minutes, then tip the mixture on to a plate.

2 Return the wok to the heat, add the remaining oil then stir in the carrots and cabbage and stir-fry for 2–3 minutes. Tip the vegetables on to the plate with the pork and shrimp.

3 Pour the stock, soy sauce and sugar into the wok and stir until the sugar has dissolved. Add the noodles, untangling them with chopsticks, and cook for about 3 minutes, until tender but still firm to the bite. Toss in the pork, shrimp, cabbage and carrots, making sure that they are thoroughly mixed.

4 Tip the noodles on to a warmed serving dish and scatter the chopped eggs over the top. Serve immediately with the lime wedges to squeeze over them.

COOK'S TIP
Fresh egg noodles are available in Chinese and South-east Asian stores.

Reserved mainly for special occasions and celebrations, such as birthdays and weddings, this is one of the national dishes of the Philippines. Packed with ingredients and topped with chopped egg, these traditional stir-fried noodles vary from region to region but are every Filipino cook's pride and joy.

Aubergine, Bitter Melon and Okra Stew Pinakbet

1 Put the okra in a large bowl, add the lime juice, toss together and leave to marinate for 30 minutes. Cut the melon in half lengthways, remove the core then cut the flesh into bitesize chunks. Put aside.

2 Meanwhile, heat the oil in a wok or a large, heavy pan, stir in the garlic and ginger and fry until fragrant. Add the shallots and fry for about 5 minutes until golden brown. Stir in the *bagnet* and fry for 1 minute, then add the *bagoong*, tomatoes and stock. Bring to the boil, reduce the heat and simmer for about 10 minutes.

3 Drain the okra and add to the pan along with the chopped aubergines and bitter melon and cook for a further 10–15 minutes until the vegetables are tender but not too soft. Season the stew with salt and pepper to taste and serve with rice.

COOK'S TIP
If you can't find *bagoong*, you could substitute it with a Filipino, Indonesian or Thai shrimp paste.

This Filipino dish is flavoured with the much-loved bagoong, *the fermented anchovy sauce, which is available in South-east Asian and Filipino supermarkets. The* bagnet *lends a rich meaty flavour to this stew, which compliments the fermented fish, resulting in a tasty main course dish.*

Serves 4–6
225g/8oz okra
juice of 1 lime
1 bitter melon
15–30ml/1–2 tbsp palm or corn oil
1–3 garlic cloves, crushed
25g/1oz fresh root ginger, grated
4 shallots, thickly sliced
350g/12oz *bagnet* (crispy fried pork belly, *see page 23*)
15–30ml/1–2 tbsp *bagoong* or 15ml/1 tbsp shrimp paste
400g/14oz can plum tomatoes
250ml/8fl oz/1 cup pork or chicken stock
1 aubergine (eggplant), cut into bitesize wedges, or 2–3 Thai aubergines, quartered
salt and ground black pepper
cooked rice, to serve

Bicolano Snake Bean Stew
Linagang sitaw

1 Heat the oil in a wok or large, heavy frying pan that has a lid. Stir in the onion, garlic, ginger, lemon grass and chillies and fry until fragrant and beginning to colour. Add the *bagoong* or shrimp paste, tamarind paste and sugar and stir in the coconut milk and lime leaves.

2 Bring the mixture to the boil, reduce the heat and toss in the whole snake beans. Partially cover the pan and cook the beans gently for 6–8 minutes until tender. Season the stew with salt and pepper to taste and sprinkle with chopped coriander to garnish. Serve with rice and extra chillies to chew on.

COOK'S TIP
If preferred, you can reduce the quantity of chillies used in the recipe to suit your taste buds and you do not have to serve the stew with extra chillies if you don't want to.

Serves 3–4

30–45ml/2–3 tbsp coconut or
   groundnut oil
1 onion, finely chopped
2–3 garlic cloves, finely chopped
40g/1½oz fresh root ginger,
   finely chopped
1 lemon grass stalk, finely chopped
4–5 red chillies, seeded and finely
   chopped
15–30ml/1–2 tbsp *bagoong* or
   15ml/1 tbsp shrimp paste
15–30ml/1–2 tbsp tamarind paste
15–30ml/1–2 tbsp palm sugar
2 x 400g/14oz cans unsweetened
   coconut milk
4 kaffir lime leaves
500g/1¼lb snake beans (yardlong
   beans)
salt and ground black pepper
1 bunch of fresh coriander (cilantro)
   leaves, chopped, to garnish

To serve
cooked rice
raw chillies

Known as Bicol, the southern Luzon peninsula in the Philippines is renowned for its fiery food, laced with hot chillies and coconut milk. In typical Bicolano style, this rich, pungent dish is hot and, believe it or not, it is served with extra chillies to chew on!

Green Papaya Salad
Atsarang papaya

Serves 4

2 green papayas, seeded and grated
4 shallots, finely sliced
1–2 red chillies, seeded, halved
    lengthways and finely sliced
150g/5oz/1 cup plump sultanas
    (golden raisins) or raisins
2 garlic cloves, crushed
25g/1oz fresh root ginger, grated
45–60ml/3–4 tbsp coconut or
    cane vinegar
50g/2oz palm sugar
1 small bunch of coriander (cilantro)

Throughout South-east Asia, unripe green mangoes and papayas are used for salads. Their tart, crunchy flesh complements spicy grilled or stir-fried dishes beautifully. This Filipino version is sweet and sour, achieving the desired balance for grilled or deep-fried pork and chicken.

1 Put the papaya, shallots, chillies, sultanas or raisins, garlic and ginger into a bowl. In a separate small bowl, mix together the coconut vinegar and sugar until the sugar has dissolved.

2 Pour the sweet vinegar over the salad and toss well together. Leave the salad to marinate for at least 1 hour or, even better, in the refrigerator overnight to allow the flavours to mingle. Serve garnished with fresh coriander leaves.

VARIATION
Use green mango or grated carrots, or you can combine the papaya with carrots for their vibrant colours.

Seaweed Salad with Green Mango
Gulamen salada

Serves 4

50g/2oz fine thread seaweed,
reconstituted in water, or
225g/8oz fresh seaweed, cut into
strips
1 green mango, grated
2–3 ripe tomatoes, skinned, seeded
and chopped
4–6 spring onions (scallions), white
parts only, sliced
25g/1oz fresh root ginger, grated
45ml/3 tbsp coconut or cane vinegar
10ml/2 tsp chilli oil
15ml/1 tbsp sugar
salt and ground black pepper

1 Bring a large pan of water to the boil, drop in the seaweed, remove from the heat and leave to soak for 15 minutes. Drain and refresh under cold running water. Using your hands, squeeze the seaweed dry.

2 Put the seaweed, mango, tomatoes, spring onions and ginger into a large bowl. In a separate bowl, mix together the coconut vinegar, chilli oil and sugar until the sugar has dissolved. Pour the dressing over the salad, toss well together and season with salt and pepper to taste. Serve as an appetizer or with grilled (broiled) meat or fish.

COOK'S TIP
Fresh and dried seaweeds are available in Chinese and South-east Asian supermarkets, but some dried varieties are available in health food stores. For this recipe, you need the fine thread seaweed available in Chinese stores.

In the Philippines, various types of seaweed are enjoyed in salads and the occasional stir-fry. Serve this salad as an appetizer or as an accompaniment to grilled meats and fish.

Twice-cooked Lapu-lapu
Escabeching lapu-lapu

1 Preheat the oven to 180°C/350°F/Gas 4. Rub the fish with salt. Heat 15ml/1 tbsp of the oil in a large frying pan, add the fish and fry on both sides for 2 minutes. Remove the fish from the pan and put aside.

2 Add the remaining oil to the pan, stir in the ginger, shallots, carrot and pepper and fry for 2–3 minutes until they begin to colour. Stir in the vinegar, soy sauce and sugar and season well with black pepper.

3 Put the fish in an ovenproof dish, spoon over the sauce and bake in the oven for 25–30 minutes. Garnish with the spring onions and serve with the lime wedges to squeeze over the fish.

Serves 3–4

1–2 fresh lapu-lapu, sea bass or red snapper, gutted and cleaned, total weight 1.2–1.3kg/2½–3lb
30ml/2 tbsp palm or groundnut (peanut) oil
25g/1oz fresh root ginger, chopped
4 shallots, finely chopped
1 large carrot, diced
1 red (bell) pepper, seeded and diced
30ml/2 tbsp coconut vinegar
30ml/2 tbsp light soy sauce
10ml/2 tsp sugar
salt and ground black pepper
4 spring onions (scallions), finely sliced, to garnish
1 lime, cut into wedges, to serve

It may seem like overkill but, in South-east Asia, it is not unusual to cook fish or meat twice to achieve the desired tender effect. In this Filipino dish from Cebu, the local fish, lapu-lapu, is first fried and then baked in a sauce. The fish itself is named after the local chief who fought Magellan during the battle of Mactan and it is, therefore, extremely popular on that island. Red snapper or sea bass are excellent substitutes.

Milk Fish Stuffed with Minced Pork and Peas
Relyenong bangus

Serves 3–4

1–2 fresh milk fish, sea bass or
    mackerel, gutted and cleaned,
    total weight 1.2–1.3kg/2½–3lb
15–30ml/1–2 tbsp palm or
    groundnut (peanut) oil
2–3 shallots, finely chopped
2 garlic cloves, finely chopped
115g/4oz minced (ground) pork
30ml/2 tbsp light soy sauce
400g/14oz can petit pois (baby
    peas), drained and rinsed
15ml/1 tbsp groundnut (peanut)
    or vegetable oil, for frying
15g/½oz/1 tbsp butter
salt and ground black pepper

To serve

45–60ml/3–4 tbsp coconut vinegar
2 red chillies, seeded and finely
    chopped

VARIATION

If you prefer a spicier filling, add
finely chopped fresh root ginger
and fresh chillies to the pan with
the garlic and the shallots.

1 Preheat the oven to 180°C/350°F/Gas 4. Put the fish on a flat surface and gently bash the body (not the head) with a rolling pin to soften the flesh and then, using your fingers, gently massage the skin away from the flesh. Be careful not to tear the skin. Using a sharp knife, make an incision on the underside of the fish, just below the gills, and squeeze the flesh from the tail end through this hole, keeping the head and backbone intact. Remove all the small bones from the flesh.

2 Heat the 15–30ml/1–2 tbsp palm or groundnut oil in a heavy frying pan, stir in the shallots and garlic and fry until they turn golden brown. Add the minced pork and fry for 2–3 minutes, and then stir in the fish flesh until mixed well together. Stir in the soy sauce and peas, and season well with salt and pepper.

3 Hold the empty fish skin in one hand and carefully stuff the fish and pork mixture back into the fish with the other hand. Secure the opening with a cocktail stick.

4 Heat the 15ml/1 tbsp groundnut or vegetable oil and the butter in a heavy frying pan and fry the stuffed fish on both sides, until well browned. Remove the fish from the pan, wrap it in a sheet of aluminium foil and place it on a baking tray. Bake in the oven for about 35 minutes to allow the flavours to combine.

6 Mix the coconut vinegar and chillies together. Remove the fish from the oven and cut it into diagonal slices. Serve with the coconut vinegar.

In this dish, the fish is bashed gently to loosen the skin, so that the flesh and bones can be removed from the fish while keeping it intact. The flesh is then cooked with pork and stuffed back into the empty fish skin.

Steamed Shellfish with Tamarind Dipping Sauce Pinakoloan na hipon

1 Scrub the lobsters, crabs, mussels and scallops or clams thoroughly under cold running water, removing any barnacles and seaweed. Rinse the prawns. Cut the spring onions into 2.5cm/1in pieces and then into fine strips.

2 Fill the bottom of two large steam pots with at least 5cm/2in water, then divide the spring onions, vinegar, garlic, ginger and peppercorns between them. Cover and bring to the boil.

3 Place the large shellfish in one steamer and the smaller shellfish in the other. (You may need to steam them in batches and top up the water if it gets low.) Cover the pots and steam the lobsters and crabs for 10 minutes and the smaller shellfish for 5 minutes, until they turn opaque and the mussel, scallops or clam shells open.

4 Transfer the cooked shellfish to a large warmed serving dish and serve with the tamarind and lime sauce, accompanied by rice and a green papaya salad.

COOK'S TIP

Take care to discard any mussel, scallop or clam shells that are open before cooking or remain closed after cooking.

Serves 4–6

2 whole lobsters, each weighing about 450g/1lb
3–4 medium crabs
24 mussels
24 scallops or clams
24 tiger prawns (shrimp)
6 spring onions (scallions)
150ml/¼ pint/⅔ cup coconut or rice vinegar
6 garlic cloves, crushed whole
about 50g/2oz fresh root ginger, finely sliced
6–8 black peppercorns

To serve

tamarind and lime dipping sauce
cooked rice
green papaya salad

Steamed, boiled or grilled and served with dipping sauces, this is one of the favourite ways of eating shellfish in the Philippines. Whether it's a snack or a main dish, the locals never seem to tire of it, cracking shells open, sharing and dipping and chatting about life.

Cured Herring Kinilaw

Serves 4

150ml/¼ pint/⅔ cup coconut vinegar
juice of 2 kalamansi limes
40g/1½oz fresh root ginger, grated
2 red chillies, seeded and finely
　sliced
8–10 herring fillets, cut into
　bitesize pieces
2 shallots, finely sliced
1 green mango, cut into julienne
　strips
1 small bunch fresh coriander
　(cilantro)
1 lime, cut into wedges
salt and ground black pepper

1 Put the coconut vinegar, lime juice, ginger and chillies in a bowl and mix together. Season the mixture with salt and pepper.

2 Put the herring fillets in a shallow dish, scatter the shallots and green mango over the top, and pour the vinegar mixture over the fish.

3 Cover with clear film (plastic wrap) and leave to marinate in the refrigerator for 1–2 hours or overnight, turning the fish several times. Serve with coriander leaves scattered over the top and lime wedges.

Generally served as an appetizer or snack in the Philippines, kinilaw can be made with many types of fish, including octopus, halibut and salmon, although mackerel and herring are particularly suitable. As with sushi or any other raw fish dish, the fish must be absolutely fresh. Cured in coconut vinegar and kalamansi lime juice, and flavoured with ginger and chillies, kinilaw is a delicious and refreshing snack.

Oxtail Braised in Peanut Sauce Kare kare

Serves 4

1.5kg/1lb 5oz oxtail, cut into
  2.5cm/1in pieces
corn or groundnut (peanut) oil
  (if necessary)
1 onion, sliced
4–5 garlic cloves, crushed whole
400g/14oz can plum tomatoes
30ml/2 tbsp *patis* (fish sauce)
2–3 bay leaves
1.5 litres/2½ pints/6¼ cups beef
  stock
40g/1½oz rice flour, dry-roasted
115g/4oz roasted unsalted peanuts,
  finely ground
1 banana heart (blossom), sliced into
  bitesize pieces
12 snake beans (yardlong beans),
  cut into 2.5cm/1in pieces
1 aubergine (eggplant), cut into
  bitesize pieces
salt and ground black pepper

To serve

cooked rice
60–90ml/4–6 tbsp *bagoong*
  (shrimp sauce)
1 firm green mango, finely sliced

1 Heat a heavy, flameproof casserole, add the oxtail pieces and cook until browned on both sides. You may need to add a little oil but generally the oxtail renders sufficient fat. Transfer the meat to a plate.

2 Heat the fat from the oxtail, adding a little oil if there is not enough, stir in the onion and garlic and fry until they begin to brown. Add the tomatoes, *patis* and bay leaves and pour in the stock.

3 Return the oxtail to the pan. Bring to the boil, reduce the heat, cover and simmer gently for 4–5 hours, until tender, adding a little extra water if necessary.

4 Skim the fat off the top and, using a slotted spoon, lift the oxtail on to a plate. Stir the rice flour and ground peanuts into the stew and whisk until fairly smooth. Add the banana heart, snake beans and aubergine and simmer for 5–6 minutes, until tender.

5 Season the stew with salt and pepper to taste. Return the oxtail to the pan and simmer for a further 5 minutes. Serve hot, with rice, a bowl of *bagoong* to spoon over the stew and slices of green mango.

VARIATIONS
This dish can also be made with meaty beef ribs or shin (shank) of veal. Powdered peanuts, available from South-east Asian supermarkets, can be used instead of the ground peanuts.

In true Spanish style, many of the Filipino stews are rich and hearty. The Filipinos love oxtail and cook it in more ways than any other country in South-east Asia. The peanuts enrich the sauce and give this dish its own character.

Beef and Chorizo Stew Pochero

1 Heat the oil in a wok with a lid or a flameproof casserole, stir in the onion, garlic and ginger and fry until they begin to brown. Add the chorizo sausages and beef and fry until they begin to brown. Add the tomatoes and pour in the stock. Bring to the boil, reduce the heat, cover and simmer gently for about 45 minutes.

2 Add the plantains and chickpeas to the stew and cook for a further 20–25 minutes, adding a little extra water if the cooking liquid reduces too much.

3 Meanwhile, heat enough oil for deep-frying in a wok or large, shallow pan. Deep-fry the bananas or plantain, in batches, for about 3 minutes, until crisp and golden brown. Remove from the pan using a slotted spoon, drain on kitchen paper then arrange in a serving dish or basket.

4 Season the stew with salt and pepper to taste and sprinkle with chopped coriander leaves to garnish. Serve with the deep-fried bananas or plantain and stir-fried greens.

This dish can be made with beef, chicken or pork, all of which are cooked the same way. In the Philippines, this dish is generally made with the small, firm saba bananas, which can be substituted by plantains.

Serves 4–6

30–45ml/2–3 tbsp groundnut (peanut) or corn oil
1 onion, chopped
2 garlic cloves, chopped
40g/1½oz fresh root ginger, chopped
2 x 175g/6oz chorizo sausages, cut diagonally into bitesize pieces
700g/1lb 9oz lean rump (round) beef, cut into bitesize pieces
4 tomatoes, skinned, seeded and quartered
900ml/1½ pints/3¾ cups beef or chicken stock
2 plantains, sliced diagonally
2 x 400g/14oz cans chickpeas, rinsed and drained
salt and ground black pepper
1 bunch fresh coriander (cilantro) leaves, chopped, to garnish

To serve

corn oil, for deep-frying
1–2 firm bananas or 1 plantain, sliced diagonally
stir-fried greens

Adobo Chicken and Pork Cooked with Vinegar and Ginger Adobo manok

Serves 4–6

30ml/2 tbsp coconut or groundnut (peanut) oil
6–8 garlic cloves, crushed whole
50g/2oz fresh root ginger, sliced into matchsticks
6 spring onions (scallions), cut into 2.5cm/1in pieces
5–10ml/1–2 tsp whole black peppercorns, crushed
30ml/2 tbsp palm or muscovado sugar
8–10 chicken thighs, or thighs and drumsticks
350g/12 oz pork tenderloin, cut into chunks
150ml/¼ pint/⅔ cup coconut or white wine vinegar
150ml/¼ pint/⅔ cup dark soy sauce
300ml/½ pint/1¼ cups chicken stock
2–3 bay leaves
salt

To serve

stir-fried greens
cooked rice

1 Heat the oil in a wok with a lid or a flameproof casserole, stir in the garlic and ginger and fry until they become fragrant and begin to colour. Add the spring onions and black pepper and stir in the sugar.

2 Add the chicken and pork to the wok or casserole and fry until they begin to colour. Pour in the vinegar, soy sauce and chicken stock and add the bay leaves. Bring to the boil, reduce the heat, cover and simmer gently for about 1 hour, until the meat is tender and the liquid has reduced.

3 Season the stew with salt to taste and serve with stir-fried greens and rice, over which the cooking liquid is spooned.

COOK'S TIP

For the best flavour, make this dish the day before eating. Leave the cooked dish to cool, put in the refrigerator overnight, then reheat the next day.

Originally from Mexico, adobo has become the national dish of the Philippines. It can be made with chicken (adobong manok), with pork (adobong baboy) or with both, as in this recipe. It can also be prepared with fish, shellfish and vegetables, as the name adobong refers to the method – cooking in lots of vinegar, ginger and garlic – not the dish itself.

Serves 3–4

6–8 small or 3 large ripe bananas
corn or vegetable oil, for deep-frying
icing (confectioners') sugar or caster
    (superfine) sugar, for dusting
coconut cream, to serve

For the batter

115g/4oz/1 cup plain (all-purpose)
    flour
5ml/1 tsp baking powder
pinch of salt
2 eggs, lightly beaten
400g/14oz can coconut milk
15ml/1 tbsp palm sugar
25g/1oz fresh root ginger, finely
    grated
50g/2oz fresh coconut, grated, or
    desiccated (dry unsweetened
    shredded) coconut

To flambé

15–30ml/1–2 tbsp sugar
rice alcohol or rum
coconut cream

Flambéed Banana Fritters
Maruya

1 First make the batter. Sift the flour, baking powder and salt into a large bowl. Make a well in the centre and drop in the beaten eggs. Gradually pour in the coconut milk, beating all the time with a whisk or wooden spoon, until the batter is smooth. Beat in the sugar, grated ginger and coconut. Leave the batter to stand for 30 minutes.

2 Cut the bananas in half and cut each half lengthways. Beat the batter again and drop in the bananas, making sure they are well coated.

3 Heat enough oil for deep-frying in a wok or deep pan. Working in batches and using a pair of tongs, lift 2–3 bananas out of the batter and lower them into the oil.

4 Fry the bananas until crisp and golden brown, then lift them out and drain on kitchen paper. Dust with icing or caster sugar and eat warm with your fingers, served with coconut cream.

5 Alternatively, to flambé the banana fritters, arrange the deep-fried bananas in a wide, heavy pan and place over a medium heat. Sprinkle the sugar over the top and toss the bananas in the pan until they are sticky and slightly caramelized. Lower the heat, pour in the rum and set alight. (Have a lid handy to smother the flames if necessary.) Spoon the rum over the bananas and serve immediately with coconut cream.

You can find deep-fried banana fritters at food stalls and cafés in Vietnam, Thailand, Malaysia, Singapore, Indonésia and the Philippines. This Filipino recipe is particularly delicious as grated ginger and coconut are added to the batter. Local rum is used to flambé the bananas, which are then served with coconut cream.

Fiesta Coconut Rice Cake
Suman

1 Put the rice in a sieve or strainer and rinse under cold running water until the water runs clear then drain. Put the rice and the coconut milk in a heavy, non-stick, shallow pan and bring to the boil, stirring to prevent the rice sticking to the bottom. Reduce the heat and simmer for 10 minutes, until the rice sticks to the back of a wooden spoon.

2 Add the sugar to the rice and stir until it dissolves. Add the ginger, spring onion, vanilla essence and lime juice. Simmer until all the liquid has been absorbed. Remove from the heat, cover and leave to steam and cool.

3 Meanwhile, put the coconut in a small, heavy frying pan and dry-fry until it turns golden brown and gives off a nutty aroma.

4 When the rice has cooled and is fairly solid, cut it into a criss-cross pattern and lift out the diamond-shaped wedges with a spatula. Place on individual squares of banana or coconut palm leaf. Sprinkle a little of the coconut over the top and serve with lime wedges to squeeze over the cakes.

The small quantity of spring onions included in the recipe give the rice cakes an interesting taste, which is much enjoyed by Filipinos. The rice cakes can be steamed in banana or palm leaves, or cooked in a heavy, non-stick pan, as in this recipe, then cut into wedges and served on coconut palm leaves.

Serves 4–6

225g/8oz/1 cup plus 30ml/2 tbsp sticky rice
600ml/1 pint/2½ cups coconut milk
225g/8oz/1 cup palm or muscovado (molasses) sugar
25g/1oz fresh root ginger, finely grated
1 spring onion (scallion), white parts only, very finely chopped
2–3 drops vanilla essence (extract)
juice of 2 kalamansi or ordinary limes

To serve

30–45ml/2–3 tbsp desiccated (dry unsweetened shredded) coconut
1 lime, cut into wedges
banana or palm leaves

Mango Ice Cream Manila manga ice cream

Serves 4–6

6 egg yolks

115g/4oz/heaped ½ cup caster (superfine) sugar

500ml/17fl oz/2¼ cups full fat (whole) or skimmed milk

350g/12oz mango flesh (about 3 mangoes)

300ml/½ pint/1¼ cups double (heavy) cream

1 In a bowl, whisk the egg yolks and sugar together until light and frothy. In a heavy pan, heat the milk until scalding and then slowly pour the milk into the egg mixture, whisking all the time. Strain the milk and egg mixture back into the rinsed pan. Heat, stirring all the time, until thickened but do not allow the mixture to boil. Leave to cool.

2 Mash the mango with a fork, or purée it in an electric blender or food processor.

3 Strain the cooled custard into a large bowl. Add the cream and whisk together. Beat in the mango purée until well mixed.

4 Pour the mixture into an ice cream maker and churn until frozen, according to the manufacturer's instructions. Alternatively, pour into a freezer container and freeze, uncovered, for 1–2 hours until beginning to set around the edges. Turn into a bowl and beat to break up the ice crystals. Return to the freezer container and repeat the beating again, then cover and freeze until firm.

COOK'S TIP

Serve the ice cream with thin slices of fresh mango to emphasize the flavours of this tropical treat.

Two of the most popular ice creams in the Philippines are made from fresh mangoes and coconuts. Ice creams are sometimes served as puddings in restaurants and at special feasts, otherwise they are enjoyed at any time of the day and in the evening at ice cream parlours and street stalls.

Iced Preserved Fruit and Legume Drink
Halo-halo

Serves 2

30ml/2 tbsp preserved sweet beans
30ml/2 tbsp preserved sugar-palm fruit
30ml/2 tbsp preserved purple yam
30ml/2 tbsp preserved macapuno coconut
crushed ice
30ml/2 tbsp condensed milk
2 lychees, stoned (pitted)
2 half moon slices ripe mango, with their skin, to decorate

Literally translated as "mixed-mixed", this is the Filipino version of Vietnam's famous rainbow drink. It is packed with fruit preserves and chilled with crushed ice, over which sweet condensed milk is poured. Known as a "working man's drink", it is really more of a snack and is well worth sampling on a hot day.

1 Divide the preserved ingredients between two tall glasses, layering them in any order you want. Fill the rest of the glass with crushed ice to 2.5cm/1in from the top. Spoon the condensed milk over the ice so that it runs down the inside of the glass.

2 Place a lychee on top of each drink. Make a small incision in the middle of each mango slice and use to decorate the glasses by securing them on the edge of the glass rim. Serve immediately, with a long-handled spoon to reach down into the depths of the preserves.

COOK'S TIP
All the preserved ingredients needed to make halo-halo are available in jars in Chinese and South-east Asian food stores.

Mango and Lime Drink
Manga at kalamansi inumin

Serves 2
4 very ripe mangoes, stoned (pitted)
15–30ml/1–2 tbsp sugar
crushed ice
juice of 1–2 kalamansi or
    ordinary limes
2 slices fresh lime, to decorate

1 Put the mango flesh in a blender or food processor and whizz to form a purée. Sweeten with sugar according to your taste. Divide the purée between two tall glasses.

2 Spoon a layer of crushed ice over the top of the mango purée then pour over the lime juice. Make a small incision in each slice of lime and use to decorate the glasses by wedging them on the edge of the rim.

3 Serve immediately, with a long spoon or a straw.

COOK'S TIP
The sweet-toothed Filipinos sometimes purée the mangoes with condensed milk, or pour the milk over the ice on top of the mango.

The tropical islands of the Philippines are home to a wide variety of different mangoes, some of which you do not see anywhere else. As there is such an abundance of ripe mangoes readily available, many are used to make either mango ice cream or this drink, which is often enjoyed at breakfast or as a refreshing snack in the heat of the day.

Fresh Ginger Tea Bandrek

Serves 4

1 litre/1¾ pints/4 cups water
40g/1½oz fresh root ginger, sliced
1–2 cinnamon sticks
5ml/1 tsp black peppercorns
30ml/2 tbsp palm sugar
115g/4oz/¾ cup coconut flesh,
    finely shredded

1 Put the water, ginger, cinnamon sticks, peppercorns and sugar into a pan and bring to the boil, stirring until the sugar has dissolved. Boil vigorously for 2 minutes, then reduce the heat and simmer for at least 15 minutes.

2 Divide the shredded coconut between four heatproof glasses and strain over the hot ginger tea. Serve immediately, with a spoon to scoop up the coconut.

COOK'S TIP

The tea improves with standing so, if convenient, you can make it in advance and reheat it before serving

Ginger tea is the preferred breakfast beverage in the Philippines as it is regarded as warming and stimulates the digestion. The traditional Filipino method of making the tea is to wrap the freshly sliced ginger in a piece of muslin (cheesecloth) and then squeeze out the juices.

Nutritional notes

Chicken and Ginger Broth with Papaya: Energy 290kcal/1219kJ; Protein 46.4g; Carbohydrate 9.8g, of which sugars 8.7g; Fat 7.5g, of which saturates 1.5g; Cholesterol 169mg; Calcium 40mg; Fibre 2.2g; Sodium 150mg.

Rice Soup with Pork and Roasted Garlic: Energy 195kcal/813kJ; Protein 14.8g; Carbohydrate 19.9g, of which sugars 3.4g; Fat 6.2g, of which saturates 1.3g; Cholesterol 37mg; Calcium 24mg; Fibre 0.8g; Sodium 399mg.

Pork Satay: Energy 360kcal/1503kJ; Protein 31.5g; Carbohydrate 11.7g, of which sugars 6.7g; Fat 21.1g, of which saturates 6.8g; Cholesterol 96mg; Calcium 40mg; Fibre 0.6g; Sodium 1048mg.

Crispy Fried Pork Belly: Energy 576kcal/2377kJ; Protein 19.2g; Carbohydrate 0.1g, of which sugars 0.1g; Fat 55.4g, of which saturates 17.7g; Cholesterol 90mg; Calcium 14mg; Fibre 0.1g; Sodium 97mg.

Spanish-style Omelette with Bitter Melon: Energy 255kcal/1064kJ; Protein 24.3g; Carbohydrate 10.5g, of which sugars 10.1g; Fat 13.2g, of which saturates 2.7g; Cholesterol 318mg; Calcium 149mg; Fibre 2.7g; Sodium 247mg.

Fried Rice with Chorizo and Fried Eggs: Energy 567kcal/2367kJ; Protein 17.7g; Carbohydrate 45.4g, of which sugars 2g; Fat 36.4g, of which saturates 11.6g; Cholesterol 225mg; Calcium 92mg; Fibre 0.6g; Sodium 1136mg.

Paella: Energy 637kcal/2666kJ; Protein 54.4g; Carbohydrate 78.3g, of which sugars 4.6g; Fat 11.6g, of which saturates 2.1g; Cholesterol 266mg; Calcium 104mg; Fibre 3.8g; Sodium 628mg.

Risotto with Stir-fried Liver: Energy 756kcal/3167kJ; Protein 49.2g; Carbohydrate 87.7g, of which sugars 33.3g; Fat 23.3g, of which saturates 4.6g; Cholesterol 423mg; Calcium 74mg; Fibre 2.3g; Sodium 197mg.

Celebration Noodles: Energy 728kcal/3069kJ; Protein 43.6g; Carbohydrate 98g, of which sugars 16.9g; Fat 20.8g, of which saturates 5g; Cholesterol 290mg; Calcium 159mg; Fibre 6.3g; Sodium 1303mg.

Aubergine, Bitter Melon and Okra Stew: Energy 323kcal/1340kJ; Protein 16.1g; Carbohydrate 9.4g, of which sugars 8.9g; Fat 24.8g, of which saturates 8.2g; Cholesterol 74mg; Calcium 118mg; Fibre 3.3g; Sodium 200mg.

Bicolano Snake Bean Stew: Energy 200kcal/840kJ; Protein 5.5g; Carbohydrate 24.4g, of which sugars 22.9g; Fat 9.7g, of which saturates 1.5g; Cholesterol 19mg; Calcium 158mg; Fibre 3.4g; Sodium 384mg.

Green Papaya Salad: Energy 232kcal/988kJ; Protein 2.5g; Carbohydrate 58.3g, of which sugars 57.6g; Fat 0.4g, of which saturates 0g; Cholesterol 0mg; Calcium 81mg; Fibre 5.5g; Sodium 19mg.

Seaweed Salad with Green Mango: Energy 75kcal/315kJ; Protein 2.4g; Carbohydrate 12g, of which sugars 11.8g; Fat 2.2g, of which saturates 0.3g; Cholesterol 0mg; Calcium 110mg; Fibre 2.8g; Sodium 85mg.

Twice-cooked Lapu-lapu: Energy 237kcal/1001kJ; Protein 38.6g; Carbohydrate 10g, of which sugars 9.1g; Fat 5.1g, of which saturates 1g; Cholesterol 69mg; Calcium 100mg; Fibre 1.7g; Sodium 720mg.

Milk Fish Stuffed with Minced Pork and Peas: Energy 397kcal/1665kJ; Protein 53.3g; Carbohydrate 12.7g, of which sugars 3.4g; Fat 15.4g, of which saturates 4.6g; Cholesterol 102mg; Calcium 116mg; Fibre 4.9g; Sodium 413mg.

Steamed Shellfish with Tamarind Dipping Sauce: Energy 312kcal/1315kJ; Protein 61g; Carbohydrate 3.4g, of which sugars 0.5g; Fat 6.1g, of which saturates 1g; Cholesterol 309mg; Calcium 193mg; Fibre 0.6g; Sodium 769mg.

Cured Herring: Energy 408kcal/1699kJ; Protein 36.4g; Carbohydrate 5.9g, of which sugars 5.7g; Fat 26.7g, of which saturates 6.6g; Cholesterol 100mg; Calcium 160mg; Fibre 1.9g; Sodium 260mg.

Oxtail Braised in Peanut Sauce: Energy 885kcal/3693kJ; Protein 85.5g; Carbohydrate 19.2g, of which sugars 8.4g; Fat 52g, of which saturates 18.5g; Cholesterol 281mg; Calcium 89mg; Fibre 5.3g; Sodium 958mg.

Beef and Chorizo Stew: Energy 583kcal/2441kJ; Protein 40.5g; Carbohydrate 35.8g, of which sugars 6.2g; Fat 31.9g, of which saturates 11.1g; Cholesterol 91mg; Calcium 104mg; Fibre 6.1g; Sodium 778mg.

Adobe Chicken and Pork Cooked with Vinegar and Ginger: Energy 270kcal/1135kJ; Protein 42.2g; Carbohydrate 9g, of which sugars 7.6g; Fat 7.4g, of which saturates 1.6g; Cholesterol 118mg; Calcium 24mg; Fibre 0.6g; Sodium 1892mg.

Flambéed Banana Fritters: Energy 407kcal/1710kJ; Protein 7.8g; Carbohydrate 53.3g, of which sugars 29.7g; Fat 19.7g, of which saturates 8.8g; Cholesterol 95mg; Calcium 95mg; Fibre 3.4g; Sodium 151mg.

Fiesta Coconut Rice Cake: Energy 323kcal/1365kJ; Protein 4.1g; Carbohydrate 76g, of which sugars 44.1g; Fat 1g, of which saturates 0.2g; Cholesterol 0mg; Calcium 56mg; Fibre 0g; Sodium 114mg.

Mango Ice Cream: Energy 466kcal/1941kJ; Protein 7.2g; Carbohydrate 35.4g, of which sugars 35.2g; Fat 33.9g, of which saturates 19.2g; Cholesterol 275mg; Calcium 167mg; Fibre 2g; Sodium 59mg.

Iced Preserved Fruit and Legume Drink: Energy 182kcal/775kJ; Protein 4.2g; Carbohydrate 39.4g, of which sugars 39.3g; Fat 2g, of which saturates 1g; Cholesterol 5mg; Calcium 94mg; Fibre 5.2g; Sodium 31mg.

Mango and Lime Drink: Energy 230kcal/987kJ; Protein 2.2g; Carbohydrate 58g, of which sugars 57.1g; Fat 0.6g, of which saturates 0.3g; Cholesterol 0mg; Calcium 44mg; Fibre 7.8g; Sodium 7mg.

Fresh Ginger Tea: Energy 120kcal/500kJ; Protein 0.9g; Carbohydrate 8.8g, of which sugars 8.8g; Fat 9.3g, of which saturates 8g; Cholesterol 0mg; Calcium 8mg; Fibre 2.1g; Sodium 5mg.

Index